Spotter's Guide to
CATS

Howard Loxton

Illustrated by David Astin, Denise Finney,
David Hurrell and David Wright

with additional illustrations by
John Gosler and Andy Martin

Contents

The editors would like to thank Elizabeth Towe for her help and advice.

Editorial Director
Bridget Gibbs

Editors
Bridget Gibbs and
Felicity Mansfield

First published in 1980 by Usborne Publishing Limited, Usborne House, 83-85 Saffron Hill, London EC1N 8RT

© 1991, 1980 by Usborne Publishing Ltd.

How to use this book

This book is an identification guide to cat breeds. Take it with you when you go out spotting or when you visit a cat show.

The cats are arranged by color to make it easier for you to look them up. The book is divided into five main sections: cats of a single overall color, cats of two colors (including two tones of the same color, such as Tabby cats), multi-colored cats, pointed cats (see page 7), and unusual cats, such as cats with curly coats or folded ears.

Pages 42 to 48 show some of the things you will see cats doing when you go out spotting. Cats are hunters, and their bodies and behavior are geared towards this way of life.

At the back of the book (pages 49 to 58) you will find information about buying and looking after a cat of your own, and about cat shows and the organizations responsible for coordinating them and recognizing new breeds.

Non-pedigree cats

Most of the illustrations in this book are of pedigree cats (see page 5), many of which you will have to go to cat shows to see. But many non-pedigree pet cats look quite similar to some breeds of pedigree cats. For example, you will soon spot a tabby cat in your neighborhood that looks very similar to a pedigree Tabby. As long as a cat you see looks very nearly the same as a pedigree type in this book, you can count it as spotted and check it off in the small circle next to the appropriate illustration.

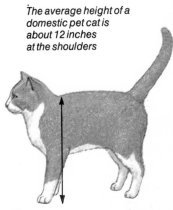

The average height of a domestic pet cat is about 12 inches at the shoulders

Size

The description next to each cat will help you to identify it. Size is not included in the descriptions because domestic cats are very similar in size whatever the breed, although individual cats may vary widely. Male cats tend to be larger than female cats, and cats that are overfed can soon get fat. Long-haired cats tend to look bigger because of their fur. The cats in this book are not drawn exactly to scale.

Scorecard

The scorecard at the end of the book gives a score for each cat spotted. Cats that you will see around your home score 5 points whereas cats that you will have to go to a show to see score 25 points. Some cats that are very rarely seen earn a score of 30 points. The scorecard also gives scores for spotting cat behavior.

Looking at cats

Pedigree cats are divided into three main groups, according to their type (build or shape). The three groups are: American Shorthairs, Longhairs and Foreign cats. In each group there are many coat colors and patterns.

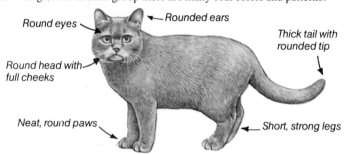

Round eyes → ← Rounded ears

Thick tail with rounded tip

Round head with full cheeks

Neat, round paws

Short, strong legs

American Shorthairs

The ideal American Shorthair has a sturdy, powerful body set on short, strong legs with neat, round paws. Its head is broad and round with a short, straight nose, full cheeks and big eyes. Its ears are small, set wide apart. American Shorthairs' tails are thick at the base and taper slightly towards the tip. Their fur is short and dense. Similar short-haired cats are bred in England and other countries in Europe.

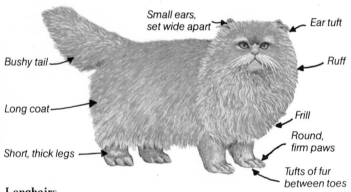

Small ears, set wide apart

Ear tuft

Bushy tail

Ruff

Long coat

Frill

Round, firm paws

Short, thick legs

Tufts of fur between toes

Longhairs

The most important feature of a Longhair (also called a Persian) is its long, silky fur. Extra-long fur forms a ruff around its face and continues in a frill between its front legs. A Longhair has a "cobby" body, large and stocky, set low on short, thick legs with round, firm paws. Its big, round head has full cheeks, a snub nose and big, round eyes. Its ears are small, set wide apart, and have long tufts of fur growing inside them. Longhairs' tails are short and bushy.

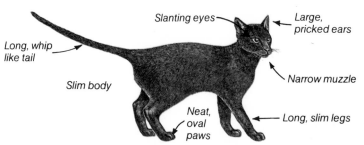

Slanting eyes

Large, pricked ears

Long, whip like tail

Narrow muzzle

Slim body

Neat, oval paws

Long, slim legs

Foreign cats

Foreign cats are also known as Orientals. The names refer to their elegant, oriental appearance and not to the country they come from. A Foreign cat has a long, fine-boned body with slender legs and a long, tapering tail. Its wedge-shaped head has large, pricked ears and slanting, almond-shaped eyes. Its fur is short and sleek.

Breeding

A pedigree cat has a recorded family tree which shows that its ancestors have been purebred for at least three generations.

Like all animals, cats inherit their shape, color and other characteristics from their parents. It is impossible to tell how many kittens a cat will have or what sex they will be, but most characteristics can be predicted if the family tree of both parents is known.

Some characteristics are dominant, that is, their presence masks the presence of other characteristics. If parents have different characteristics, most of their kittens will show the ones that are dominant. Tabby markings are a dominant characteristic, which is why there are so many Tabbies and cats with some tabby markings.

Dominant coloring

Tabby parent

Black parent

Tabby kittens

Some characteristics are only carried by one sex. For example, Tortoiseshell cats are nearly always female.

Occasionally, a kitten is born with a completely new characteristic. The curly coat of the Rex cats is an example of this. The first Rex cat was born in a litter of ordinary kittens produced by a shorthaired farm cat.

5

Coat colors and markings

A cat's coat is made up of soft, downy underfur, which keeps it warm, and a protective layer of coarser fur called a topcoat. The coat can be various colors, and it may be self-colored (plain) or marked with spots, stripes or patches. A cat's whiskers match or tone with its coat color. Whiskers are long, sensitive bristles on cats' faces that help them "feel" their way around, especially at night.

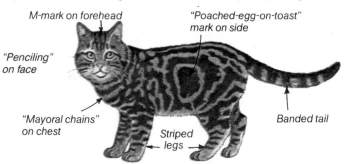

"M-mark on forehead

"Penciling" on face

"Mayoral chains" on chest

"Poached-egg-on-toast" mark on side

Banded tail

Striped legs

Classic Tabby markings are very common markings for a cat's coat. This pattern includes rings around the legs and tail, stripes across the chest called "mayoral chains," fine lines on the side of the face called "penciling" and an M-shaped mark on the forehead. There is also a mark on the cat's side that looks like a poached egg on toast, and another mark across the shoulders that looks like a butterfly.

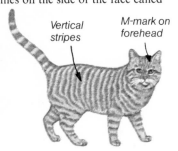

Vertical stripes

M-mark on forehead

Mackerel Tabby markings are less common; they are hardly ever seen on Longhairs. With this pattern, the Classic Tabby's body markings are replaced by narrow vertical stripes running from the spine down to the belly.

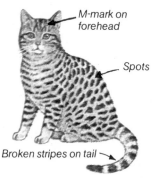

M-mark on forehead

Spots

Broken stripes on tail

Spotted Shorthairs' markings developed from Mackerel Tabby markings. In this coat pattern, the Mackerel Tabby's stripes are broken up into clearly defined spots.

Some useful words

White blaze

Red blaze

Brown coat

Pinkish-brown paw pads

Pinkish-brown nose leather

Blaze. A blaze is a wide flash of a contrasting color down the center of a cat's face. Blazes are often light-colored.

Nose leather and paw pads. Nose leather is the skin at the end of a cat's nose. Paw pads are the cushion-like pads of skin under its paws. Nose leather and paw pads are usually the same color. They match or tone with the cat's coat color.

Dark ears

Dark mask

Pale coat

Dark tail

Dark paws

Points. Some cats, such as Siamese cats, have pale coats with points of a contrasting color. The points are the legs, paws, tail, ears and mask (face).

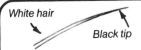

White hair

Black tip

Red hair

Black bands

Tipping. Some cats have tipped fur. This means that the hairs are of one color with a tip of a contrasting color. Chinchillas, for example, have white fur tipped with black.

Ticking. Abyssinian cats have ticked fur. Their coats look slightly speckled because the main color of each hair is broken up by two or three bands of a contrasting color.

7

Red cats

Red cats have rich, orangey-red fur. Their coats should not be ginger or sandy-colored, but should have a deep, orangey or coppery tinge.

Red Burmese ▶

All Burmese cats are playful and elegant. They are fairly heavily built for Foreign cats. This variety has a light tangerine coat, sometimes with faint tabby markings. Golden yellow eyes.

Ears are tufted ⟶

◀ Red or Sorrel
Abyssinian

A Foreign cat with a ticked top coat. Each hair is a coppery red, with bands of chocolate brown. Its underfur is apricot. Green, gold or hazel eyes, outlined in black.

Tail has a solid chocolate-brown tip

Long, silky ruff

Red Self Longhair ▶

This longhaired cat's coat should be an even color all over, but may still have tabby markings. Its body is low and sturdy, its legs are short. Orange or copper eyes.

Short bushy tail

Black cats

Black cats were once associated with witchcraft, so some people consider them unlucky. Others think they bring good luck. Black cats must not have any white hairs in their coats.

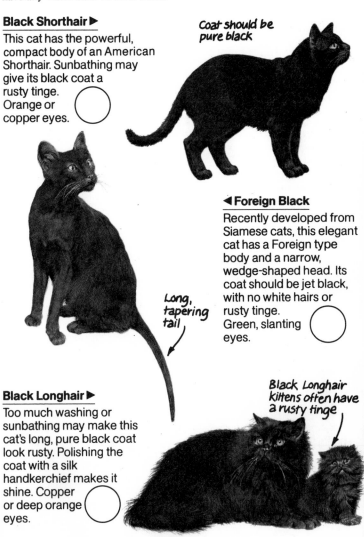

Black Shorthair ▶

This cat has the powerful, compact body of an American Shorthair. Sunbathing may give its black coat a rusty tinge. Orange or copper eyes.

Coat should be pure black

◀ Foreign Black

Recently developed from Siamese cats, this elegant cat has a Foreign type body and a narrow, wedge-shaped head. Its coat should be jet black, with no white hairs or rusty tinge. Green, slanting eyes.

Long, tapering tail

Black Longhair ▶

Too much washing or sunbathing may make this cat's long, pure black coat look rusty. Polishing the coat with a silk handkerchief makes it shine. Copper or deep orange eyes.

Black Longhair kittens often have a rusty tinge

9

Blue cats

Blue cats' fur is blue-gray. Blue is a weak form of black in cats. Blue cats often have gentle natures.

◀ British Blue

A good example of an American Shorthair. This cat has a low, stocky body and a broad, round head with big cheeks. Its blue coat is lightly ticked on the shoulders, giving it a harsh, frosty look. Rich orange, yellow or copper eyes.

Feet have a silvery sheen

Russian Blue ▶

A small, dainty cat of Foreign type. Its ears are large and paper-thin. Its silvery blue coat is short and thick. Quiet and sweet-natured. Almond-shaped green eyes.

Coat is dense, but very silky, like sealskin

Large ears

Heart-shaped face

◀ Korat

This strong, medium-sized cat comes from Thailand, where its name means "good fortune." Its glossy silver-blue coat is tipped with silver. Unusually large, bright green eyes.

Blue Abyssinian ▶

A lithe, muscular cat of Foreign type. Its underfur is pale cream or oatmeal, its top coat blue, ticked with a deeper steel blue. An uncommon variety. Amber, hazel or green eyes.

Light shading on the muzzle is common →

← *Oatmeal-colored underparts*

Back and tail are only slightly darker than the rest of the coat

◀ Blue Burmese

Burmese cats have a heavier build than most Foreign cats, but all are elegant and have fine coats. This variety has a silver-gray coat. Its face, ears and feet have a pale silver sheen. Yellow eyes.

Blue Longhair ▶

Its coat can be any shade of blue, but should be a very even color all over. The kittens may be born with tabby markings; these disappear later on. Copper or orange eyes.

Small, tufted ears, set well apart ↗

← *Short legs*

11

Lilac cats

Lilac cats were first produced by breeding together blue and chocolate cats. Their coats are a delicate dove-gray, with a pinkish tinge.

Foreign Lilac ▶

A graceful cat of Foreign type. First produced by breeding Havana and Lilac-point Siamese cats. Its coat is an even frosty gray, tinged with pink. Green eyes.

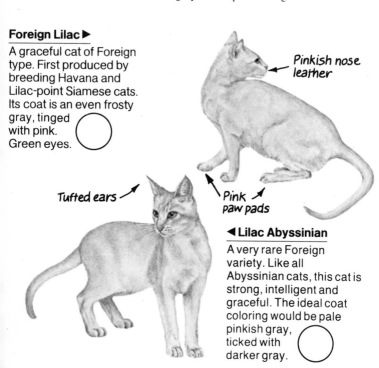

Pinkish nose leather

Tufted ears

Pink paw pads

◀ Lilac Abyssinian

A very rare Foreign variety. Like all Abyssinian cats, this cat is strong, intelligent and graceful. The ideal coat coloring would be pale pinkish gray, ticked with darker gray.

Lilac Burmese ▶

Fairly thickset for a Foreign cat. Its coat is a pale lilac, often darker on its ears and mask. The kittens have shell-pink noses and paw pads, which turn lavender-pink. Golden yellow eyes.

Ears are set wide apart

Cream cats

Cream cats' fur may be any shade of cream that does not have a "hot" (orange) tinge. Cream is a weak form of red in cats.

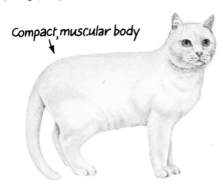

Compact, muscular body

◀ Cream Shorthair

This pale cream American Shorthair is hard to breed without tabby markings. Cream kittens born with stripes may lose their markings, but these can return.
Orange or copper eyes.

Cream Burmese ▶

An elegant Foreign cat with a rich cream coat. Faint tabby markings are allowed on its face, but not on its sides or belly. Pink nose and paw pads. Golden yellow eyes.

Dark shading on the ears

No markings are allowed on the coat

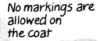

◀ Cream Longhair

A Longhair cat with a pale to medium cream coat. Cream Longhairs are bred with White Longhairs to stop the cream from becoming too hot. This can result in Cream cats with too many white hairs. Deep copper eyes.

13

White cats

White cats should be pure white, without traces of colored markings. White cats with blue eyes tend to be deaf, and should not breed with other deaf cats.

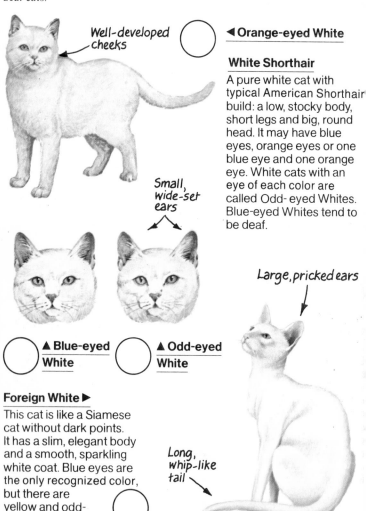

Well-developed cheeks

◀ **Orange-eyed White**

White Shorthair

A pure white cat with typical American Shorthair build: a low, stocky body, short legs and big, round head. It may have blue eyes, orange eyes or one blue eye and one orange eye. White cats with an eye of each color are called Odd-eyed Whites. Blue-eyed Whites tend to be deaf.

Small, wide-set ears

Large, pricked ears

▲ **Blue-eyed White**

▲ **Odd-eyed White**

Foreign White ▶

This cat is like a Siamese cat without dark points. It has a slim, elegant body and a smooth, sparkling white coat. Blue eyes are the only recognized color, but there are yellow and odd-eyed Foreign Whites.

Long, whip-like tail

14

Yellow stains on the coat can be removed by powdering

◀ **Blue-eyed White**

White Longhair

A pure white cat. It should be the typical Longhair shape, but its body, nose and ears are often too long and its head too narrow. It may have blue eyes, orange eyes or odd-colored eyes (one blue and one orange). Blue eyes are linked to deafness in white cats.

Tufted ears

Full cheeks

▲ **Orange-eyed White**

▲ **Odd-eyed White**

Chinchilla ▶

An unusually dainty Longhair. Its chin, ear tufts, belly and chest are pure white. The rest of its coat is tipped with black, making the coat seem to sparkle. Emerald or blue-green eyes and brick red nose are both outlined in black.

Eyes and tip of nose are outlined in black

Chinchilla kittens may be born with tabby markings or a smoky look

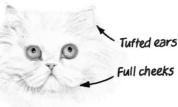

15

Brown cats

The color of brown cats' fur ranges from a warm chestnut to the color of plain (dark) chocolate.

Havana ▶

So called because it is the color of a Havana cigar. Rich brown coat, without markings. Gentle cat with a wistful look. Foreign type. Green eyes.

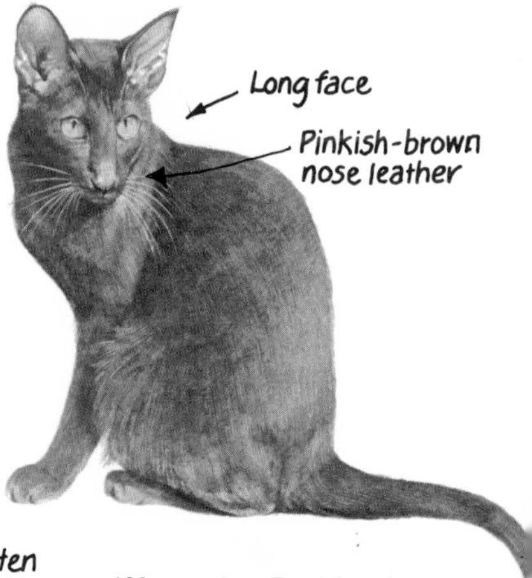

Long face

Pinkish-brown nose leather

Ear tufts

There is often a dark line down the spine

◀ Normal or Ruddy Abyssinian

The first Abyssinian cat to be bred. Ruddy brown coat, ticked with black or dark brown. Foreign type. Amber, green or hazel eyes.

Has a heavier build than other Burmese cats

Chocolate Burmese ▶

Milk chocolate colored coat with darker brown points. Golden eyes.

Brown Burmese ▶

Seal brown coat, without shading. Golden eyes.

wo-colored cats

vo-colored cats have coats of either two different colors, or two tones of
the same basic color. The colors may merge softly together, or they may
appear in separate patches or clear patterns.

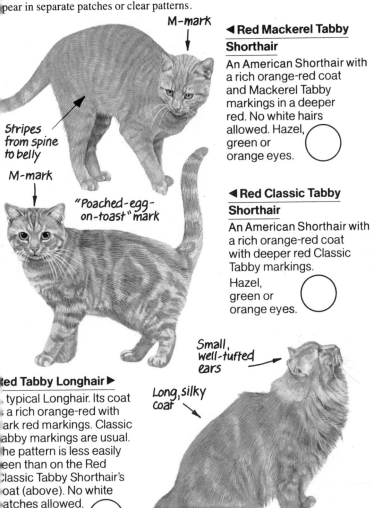

M-mark

Stripes
from spine
to belly

M-mark

"Poached-egg-
on-toast" mark

Small,
well-tufted
ears

Long, silky
coat

◀ Red Mackerel Tabby
Shorthair

An American Shorthair with
a rich orange-red coat
and Mackerel Tabby
markings in a deeper
red. No white hairs
allowed. Hazel,
green or
orange eyes.

◀ Red Classic Tabby
Shorthair

An American Shorthair with
a rich orange-red coat
with deeper red Classic
Tabby markings.
Hazel,
green or
orange eyes.

ed Tabby Longhair ▶

typical Longhair. Its coat
is a rich orange-red with
ark red markings. Classic
abby markings are usual.
he pattern is less easily
een than on the Red
lassic Tabby Shorthair's
oat (above). No white
atches allowed.
arge copper
yes.

17

Face has
tabby markings

◄ Red Spotted Shorthair

An American Shorthair breed
from the Red Mackerel
Tabby Shorthair (above).
Its spots should be well-
defined, and not look like
broken stripes. Red coat
with spots of a
deeper red.
Brilliant copper
eyes.

Face has
patches
of color

White blaze

Red and White Bi-color Shorthair ►

Not more than half of this
cat's coat may be white,
and not more than two-
thirds red. British Shorthair
build. Orange,
yellow or
copper eyes

White blaze

◄ Red and White Bi-color Longhair

Its coat is patched in red
and white in the same
proportions as the Red
and White Bi-color
Shorthair (above).
Longhair build.
Round copper or
orange eyes.

Short, thick legs

18

Turkish Cat ▶

A sturdy, long-bodied cat from Turkey. Has a shorter coat, longer face and less cobby body than most Longhairs. Chalk white coat with auburn (reddish brown) markings on its face and tail. Round amber eyes.

White blaze

Back often has a reddish tinge

Faint auburn rings on tail

◀ Black and White Bi-color Shorthair

This cat's coat can be up to two-thirds black, and up to one-half white. The black areas must be distinct, without stray white hairs. American Shorthair build. Orange or copper eyes.

White blaze

Black and White Bi-color Longhair ▶

A Longhair with the same coloring as the Black and White Bi-color Shorthair (above). These cats were once known as "Magpies." Bi-color cats are often bigger than other Longhairs. Copper eyes.

Small, tufted ears, set well apart

Full tail

19

British Tipped Shorthair ▶

Similar in coloring to the Chinchilla (page 15). Its top coat and underfur are white, but the top coat is tipped with black. Broad, round head. American Shorthair type.
Green eyes.

Eyes and tip of nose are outlined in black

Strong tipping on back and tail

◀ Smoke Shorthair

This American Shorthair has a black top coat and pale silver underfur, which shows when it moves. The fur must have no white hairs. Black nose and paw pads.
Orange or yellow eyes.

Black Smoke Longhair ▶

A longhaired cat with ash-white underfur. The top coat is ash-white, shading to black at the tips. Its ruff, ear tufts and sides are silvery. The kittens may be born black or blue.
Orange or copper eyes.

Silvery ear tufts

Very long, pale ruff

Silver Tabby Shorthair ▶

Beautiful silver coat with black markings. Either Classic or Mackerel Tabby markings. Gentle, affectionate cat of American Shorthair type. Brick red or black nose leather. Green or hazel eyes.

▼ Silver Classic Tabby Shorthair

▲ Silver Mackerel Tabby Shorthair

White hairs are not allowed in the coat

◀ Silver Spotted Shorthair

An American Shorthair cat developed from Silver Mackerel Tabby Shorthairs. Its coat is silver with black spots. Tabby markings on its head. Green or hazel eyes.

Tail may have spots or broken rings

Silver Tabby Longhair ▶

One of the most difficult longhaired cats to breed. Its pale silver coat must have clearly-defined black markings. Classic pattern only. The kittens are born almost all black. Green or hazel eyes.

Well-tufted ears

Full, silvery ruff

21

Short, dense coat with colors merging softly

◀ Blue-Cream Shorthair

The blue and cream in this American Shorthair's coat merge softly together. White fur and tabby markings are not allowed. Cats of this breed are almost always female. Copper, orange or yellow eyes.

Blue-Cream Longhair ▶

The few males of this breed are sterile (cannot breed) so females are mated with Blue or Cream Longhair males. This cat's coat is soft and silky; the blue and cream merge in a pattern rather like shot silk. Deep copper or orange eyes.

Fur colors should not appear in separate patches, but merge together

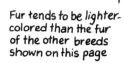

Fur tends to be lighter-colored than the fur of the other breeds shown on this page

◀ Blue-Cream Burmese

Its body is elegant, but quite thickset for a Foreign cat. Very playful. As with other Blue-Cream breeds, cats of this breed are almost always female. Golden yellow eyes.

Blue and White Bi-color
Shorthair ▶

This compact, muscular Shorthair is fairly rare. Its coat may be up to two-thirds blue and up to one-half white. Brilliant copper or orange eyes.

White blaze

Short, thick coat

Thick, silky ruff and frill

◀ Blue and White
Bi-color Longhair

Not often seen. A Longhair with silky, flowing fur. Up to a half of its coat may be white, and up to two-thirds blue. Deep orange or copper eyes.

The pale underfur shows clearly when the cat moves

Blue Smoke Longhair ▶

A beautiful longhaired cat with an unusual coat. Its underfur is ash-white, and its top coat blue, shading to silver on its sides. Its mask and feet are blue, and its frill and ear tufts silver. The kittens are born all blue. Orange or copper eyes.

Extra-long frill

23

Cream Spotted Shorthair ▶

A rare American Shorthair with a pale cream coat patterned in well-defined cream spots. It may have tabby markings on its head. Orange or copper eyes.

Tabby markings on face

Spots or broken rings on the tail

◀ Cream and White Bi-color Shorthair

Up to one-half of this American Shorthair's coat may be white, and up to two-thirds cream. There must not be any stray white hairs in the cream patches. Rare. Brilliant copper or orange eyes.

Cream and White Bi-color Longhair ▶

This cat's coat has areas of white and cream in the same proportions as the Cream and White Bi-color Shorthair (above). No tabby markings allowed. Longhair build. Deep orange or copper eyes.

Face is patched with cream and white

All Cameo cats have long, white ear tufts

◄ Shell Cameo

Cameo cats, like Chinchilla and Smoke cats, have white underfur with a tipped top coat. This is the palest of the Cameo cats. Its white top coat is tipped with pale cream or red, giving the fur a rose-pink haze. Longhair build. Rich copper eyes with pink rims.

Shaded Cameo ►

This is a darker form of the Shell Cameo. Its white top coat is lightly tipped with red, so that the coat looks a reddish-pink. Rich copper eyes with pink rims.

Red tipping gives coat a sparkling appearance

Dark mask

◄ Smoke Cameo

This is the darkest of the Cameo cats. At first glance, its coat looks all red, because the top coat is tipped with red, but the white underfur shows when it moves. Long, silky coat. Rich copper eyes with pink rims.

Brown Classic Tabby
Shorthair ▶

Sable brown or rich brown coat with black Classic Tabby markings. Orange, hazel or deep yellow eyes.

"Poached-egg-on-toast" mark

Vertical stripes

◀ Brown Mackerel Tabby
Shorthair

Black Mackerel Tabby markings on a rich brown or sable brown coat. A rare American Shorthair. Orange, hazel or deep yellow eyes.

Spots on the spine must not join up in a line

Brown Spotted
Shorthair ▶

Has the sturdy build and short, close coat of an American Shorthair. Its coat is brown with lots of clear black spots. Orange, hazel or deep yellow eyes.

Bronze Oriental Spotted Tabby ▶

This elegant, medium-sized Foreign cat was bred from Siamese cats. It looks a bit like the cats seen in Ancient Egyptian art. Its fine coat is bronze colored, with rich chocolate brown spots. Other colors are being developed. Very friendly; loves attention. Green eyes with black rims.

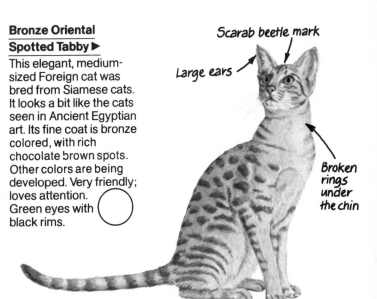

Scarab beetle mark

Large ears

Broken rings under the chin

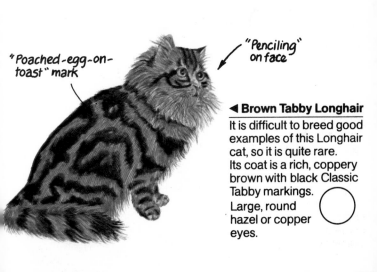

"Poached-egg-on-toast" mark

"Penciling" on face

◀ Brown Tabby Longhair

It is difficult to breed good examples of this Longhair cat, so it is quite rare. Its coat is a rich, coppery brown with black Classic Tabby markings. Large, round hazel or copper eyes.

27

Multi-colored cats

Multi-colored cats must not have strong tabby markings. Most of the cats on this page and the facing page are Tortoiseshell cats (often called Torties, for short). Male Tortoiseshell cats are very rare; they are almost always sterile (unable to breed).

Red blaze

▲ Tortoiseshell Shorthair

This attractive American Shorthair has a black coat with well-defined patches of red and cream. Almost always female. A female Tortoiseshell mated with a black or red male cat may have tortoiseshell, cream and black kittens. Orange or copper eyes.

Black kitten (male or female)

Tortoiseshell kitten (female)

White blaze

◄ Tortoiseshell and White Shorthair

A white cat with patches of red, cream and black. There should be more tortoiseshell areas than white, with colored patches on its head, ears, tail, back and sides. Very affectionate. American Shorthair build. Orange, hazel or copper eyes.

Tortoiseshell Longhair ▶

A lively, intelligent Longhair. Its coat has evenly distributed and well broken up patches of red, cream and black. The males are usually sterile (cannot breed). Copper or deep orange eyes.

Extra-long frill

White blaze on face

◀ Tortoiseshell and White Longhair

Also known as the Calico Cat. It must have some white on its face, chest, legs and feet. The rest of its coat has separate patches of red, cream and black. Always female. Deep orange or copper eyes.

Chocolate Tortie Burmese ▶

This cat's coat is a mixture of various shades of chocolate and red. Other Tortie (short for Tortoise-shell) Burmese include the Brown/Normal Tortie Burmese, from which this cat was first bred. Foreign type. Yellow eyes.

Patches of color in the coat are not clearly defined

29

Mongrel cats

The cats on this page are mongrels–cats with parents of mixed breed. Tabby cats that are not pure-bred often have white patches; you are very likely to see them in your neighborhood.

Red Tabby and White ▶

Pure-bred Red Tabbies should not have patches of white fur, and pure-bred Bi-colored cats should not have strong tabby markings, so this cat has to be classed as a mongrel.

White patches

Mongrel tabbies often have a white chest and paws

◀ Silver Tabby and White

This pretty shorthaired cat might win a special non-pedigree class at a cat show (see page 58). However, it could not enter a class for Silver Tabbies because of its white patches.

Brown Tabby and White ▶

Since it has a white ruff as well as tabby stripes, this longhaired cat does not belong to any accepted cat breed. Tabby markings often turn up in litters of mongrel kittens.

Pointed cats

Pointed cats have white, off-white or cream coats with points of a contrasting color. The points are the legs, paws, tail, ears and mask. Kittens are white all over when born and the points take several months to develop fully.

Seal-point Siamese ▶

The first variety of Siamese to be recognized. Very popular. Its coat is cream, shading to fawn on its back, with seal brown points. Siamese cats' coats tend to darken with age. Foreign type. Sapphire blue eyes.

Dark shading often develops on back but is not desirable

Kitten at four weeks of age; its points are starting to develop

Kittens are white all over when born

Blue-point Siamese ▶

A popular and attractive cat with pale blue points and an icy white coat, shading to light blue on its back. Tends to be more placid than other Siamese cats. Foreign type. Sapphire blue eyes.

Whip-like tail

◀ Chocolate-point Siamese

Has an ivory coat with milk chocolate colored points. The kittens may take up to one year to gain their full coloring. Foreign type. Sapphire blue eyes.

Like all Siamese cats, it has a very fine, close-textured coat

Coat does not usually darken with age

◄ Lilac-point Siamese

Intelligent and demanding, like all Siamese cats. Its points are pinkish-gray; the rest of the coat is off-white, shading to a pale pinkish-gray on its back. Foreign type. Blue eyes, sometimes paler than those of other Siamese cats.

Fine, colored lines called "tracings" run from the ears to the mask

Red-point Siamese ►

Originally bred from Seal-point Siamese cats and Red Tabby Shorthairs. Its clear white coat shades to apricot on its back. Reddish-gold points. Like all Siamese cats, it is very "talkative"; its voice is loud and quite harsh. Foreign type. Vivid blue eyes.

Tabby stripes may appear on the mask, legs and tail

◄ Cream-point Siamese

A delicately colored cat with some tabby markings. Its face and legs are the color of cream, and its nose, ears and tail are a warm apricot. The rest of the coat is white. Foreign type. Vivid blue eyes.

Tortie-point Siamese ▶

This variety of Siamese
cat is always female. Its
points have patches of red
and/or cream, with either
blue, lilac, seal or chocolate.
The rest of the coat is
cream or fawn.
Foreign type.
Blue eyes.

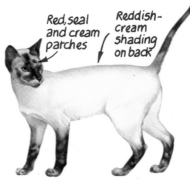

Red, seal
and cream
patches

Reddish-
cream
shading
on back

Ringed tail with
a solid colored tip

◀ Tabby-point Siamese

Once called the Shadow-
or Lynx-point Siamese,
this cat has a pale coat
with tabby markings
instead of colored points.
The markings appear in any
of the usual Siamese
colors.
Foreign type.
Blue eyes.

Dark spots
on the
whisker-
pads

Seal-point Himalayan or
Seal Colorpoint▶

Himalayans (called
Colorpoints in Britain) are
Longhairs with Siamese-
type coloring. This one
has a long cream coat and
seal brown points. It must
not have a long nose or
any other Foreign type
characteristics.
Clear, bright
blue eyes.

Broad,
round head

Low,
sturdy body

Chocolate-point Himalayan or Chocolate Colorpoint ▶

This longhaired cat's Siamese-type points are a warm, milk chocolate color. The rest of the coat is ivory; it seldom darkens with age. Clear, bright blue eyes.

Large, clear blue eyes

Small, well-tufted ears, set well apart

Short, full tail

◀ Blue-point Himalayan or Blue Colorpoint

This cat's points are blue; its stomach and chest are pure white, and the rest of its coat is a cold, bluish white. The coat may darken with age. Longhair type. Clear, bright blue eyes.

Lilac-point Himalayan or Lilac Colorpoint ▶

Its coat should be a magnolia color, without shading. The coat seldom darkens with age. Its points are frosty gray, tinged with pink, and its nose and paw pads are lavender-pink. Longhair type. Clear, bright blue eyes.

Long, thick, soft coat

◄Flame-point Himalayan or Red Colorpoint

Gentle and affectionate, like all Colorpoints. Its coat is a creamy white, with sandy orange points. Longhair type. Bright, china-blue eyes.

Cream-point Himalayan or Cream Colorpoint►

Colorpoints are becoming very popular; they are being bred in various new colors. This variety has a white coat with rich cream to apricot points. Longhair type. Blue eyes.

Long, silky coat

Round cheeks

Ear tufts

◄Tortie-point Himalayan or Tortie Colorpoint

Its coat is cream with seal, red and/or cream points. The points do not develop their full color until the second year. This variety is always female. Longhair type. Blue eyes.

Round, wide head

White "gauntlets" run up the back legs to a point at the heel

◀ Seal-point Birman

According to legend, Birmans once guarded the temples of Burma. They are stocky, long-bodied cats with round, wide heads. Their fur is long and silky (but not as thick as true Longhairs' coats). This variety has a creamy white coat with seal brown points. Intelligent and affectionate. Blue eyes.

Long, bushy tail

Blue-point Birman ▶

Just like the Seal-point Birman (above), except that its points are blue-gray. A bright, lively pet. Birman kittens are born pale all over; their points develop after several weeks. Slate gray nose. Blue eyes.

White "gauntlets"

White "gloves"

Large, pointed ears

Long, full tail

◀ Seal-point Balinese

This medium-sized, grace-ful cat is really a longhaired Siamese cat and is not Longhair in type. It has a pale coat with seal brown, Siamese-type points. Balinese cats are also bred in other Siamese cat colors. Blue eyes.

Unusual cats

The cats on pages 37 to 41 belong to unusual or recently-developed breeds. Many of them have been bred in the USA and are not often seen in other countries at the present time.

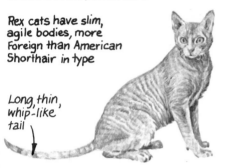

Rex cats have slim, agile bodies, more Foreign than American Shorthair in type

Long, thin, whip-like tail

◄ Cornish Rex

"Rex" is the name given to the waved or rippled texture of this cat's fur. Even its whiskers and eyebrows are curly. This breed first appeared by chance in a litter of ordinary Shorthairs in Cornwall (UK) Runs very fast. Any color.

Devon Rex ►

This dainty, pixie-faced cat first turned up in a litter of farm kittens in Devon (UK). Its softly waved coat is thinner than that of the Cornish Rex (above). Affectionate and playful. Large, wide-set eyes. Any color.

Big "batwing" ears

Crinkled whiskers (these tend to snap off)

Arched back

Wedge-shaped head

◄ Chocolate-point Si-Rex

This Si-Rex cat is a cross between a Devon Rex and a Siamese cat. Si-Rex cats have pale, curly coats with Siamese points in all the usual Siamese-type colors. Lively and independent. Blue eyes.

Broad, round rump

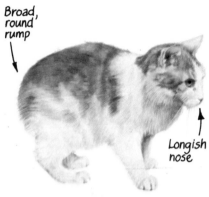

◀ Manx Cat

Manx Cats are named after the Isle of Man, one of the places where they first appeared. This variety, sometimes called a Rumpy, has no trace of a tail. It has a short back, high hindquarters and long back legs, and walks in rabbit-like hops. It has thick underfur and a soft top coat.
Manx cats can be any color.

Longish nose

"Rumpy" kitten

Manx cats' litters may include kittens with tails, "stumpy" kittens and completely tailless kittens

"Stump"

Stumpy Manx ▶

This variety of Manx Cat has a very short tail. It is less likely to suffer from the spine faults and bowel troubles that some completely tailless Manx Cats get. Otherwise, it is just the same.
Makes a good pet. Any color.

Chubby cheeks

Round rump, with no sign of a tail ↙

◀ Cymric

This breed of cat is identical to the tailless Manx Cat, except that it has a long coat. May be any color or pattern, with eyes to match.

Usually crouches, so its long back legs look shorter than they are ↓

Japanese Bobtail ▶

An ancient breed from Japan with a muscular, narrow body. Its traditional coloring is red, black and white. The coat is soft and easy to groom. Its tail is very short, carried curled up. It has slanting eyes, strong cheek-bones and very long back legs.

The ears are hard to clean properly because they are folded ➡

◀ Scottish Fold

This breed was developed from an accidental breeding in Scotland. The kittens are born with ordinary, pricked ears, which droop as they grow older. Many breeders disapprove of breeding cats with such deformiti... American Shorthair type. Any color or pattern.

40

Sphynx ▶

This odd-looking cat has practically no fur on its body. It has short, velvety fur on its face and back and light, downy fur on its legs and paws. Catches cold easily.
Foreign type.
Any color.
Golden eyes.

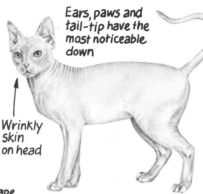

Ears, paws and tail-tip have the most noticeable down

Wrinkly skin on head

Similar in shape to the Turkish Cat

Bushy tail

Longish face

◀ Maine Coon

So-called because its fur looks like a raccoon's coat. This old breed from the USA is heavily built with a shaggy coat. It has long hair on its belly, a bushy tail and full "breeches," but quite a short ruff. Gentle.
Green, gold, blue or copper eyes.

American Wire Hair ▶

A lively, inquisitive cat bred from a wiry-haired cat born in a litter of ordinary farm kittens. The fur on its head, sides and tail is harsh and crinkled. The fur on its underparts is softer. Similar in type to an American shorthair. Any color.

Crinkly whiskers and eyebrows

Tufted ears
with dark tips

◄ Somali

A longhaired version of
the Abyssinian cat. Its coat
can be an orangey-brown
with black ticking, or a
warm red with chocolate
brown ticking. Alert
and lively. Gold
or green
eyes.

A dark line
runs down the
spine to the tip
of the tail

Coat shines
like patent
leather

Bombay ►

This muscular, medium-
sized cat was bred from
Burmese cats and short-
haired cats. Its black coat
is short, fine and very
shiny.
Gold or deep
copper eyes.

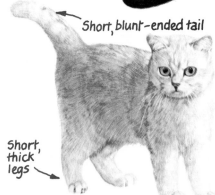

Short, blunt-ended tail

Short,
thick
legs

◄ Exotic Shorthair

This breed was carefully
developed in the USA
from shorthaired and
longhaired cats. A
beautiful cat with medium-
length fur (very easy to
groom), a short, sturdy
body and a broad head.
Any Longhair color
or pattern,
with eyes to
match.

Cat behavior

When you go out spotting cats, you can also watch how they behave. Pages 42 to 48 show some of the things you can look out for. Notice how flexible a cat's body is and how quickly and quietly it can move. This is because cats are naturally hunters and they catch their prey by stealthily stalking and surprising it.

Jumping down ▶

Cats can jump down from quite high places without damage. Their flexible skeleton and cushioned paw pads absorb the shock of landing. The position of tail, head and legs is very important for balance.

Legs outstretched for landing

◀ Jumping up

For their size, cats can jump higher and spring across much wider gaps than people can. With their strong hind legs, and hind-paws that give them a firm push off, they can spring up from a sitting position.

Climbing ▶

Cats are excellent climbers. Their claws and the rough surface of their paw pads give them a good grip.

Sharp claws help cat to climb →

Sense of touch ▶

The cat's paw pads are very sensitive to touch and pressure. Cats use their paws to investigate strange objects and to touch prey to see if it is dead.

Cats test strange objects with their paws

◀ Sharpening claws

Cats have sharp claws for killing prey and for climbing. The claws stay sharp because the outer layer comes off with wear. Cats often scratch against trees or other hard surfaces to help remove this outer shell. Scratching trees is also a way in which cats mark out their territory.

Eating grass ▶

Cats often eat grass, which helps their digestion. Also, cats swallow fur when they wash, which can collect in balls in their stomach. Eating grass helps make them vomit to get rid of these fur balls.

Sleeping and stretching

Sleeping ▶

Cats spend a lot of time sleeping, often in unlikely places, perched on ledges or parked cars. This is very light sleep, called "catnapping," from which the cat can wake instantly. Cats only sleep deeply when they feel secure.

◀ Arching back

On waking after a deep sleep, cats go through a amazing routine of stretching movements t loosen their joints and prepare them for action First, the back is arched right up like this.

Stretching front legs ▶

Next, the cat stretches out its front legs as far as they will go, forcing its bottom up in the air as it does so.

◀ Stretching back legs

Finally, each back leg is raised in turn and stretched out behind as far as it will go.

Washing

The left paw is used to wash the left side of the head

◀ Washing face and ears

Cats wash their face and ears with their front paws. The paw is licked to make it damp, then wiped around the ear, over the head, and down the face over the eye. This is repeated several times, with each paw washing one side of the head.

Washing side of body ▶

To wash and groom the side of its body, a cat stretches itself out like this. It uses its teeth to tease out any burrs or knots in the fur.

This washing position is sometimes called the "Yoga position"

◀ Washing hindquarters

A cat can bend almost double to wash its hind-quarters and the base of its tail. It twists its body to balance with one leg in the air. Its rough tongue is used to comb as well as wash its fur.

Hunting

Stalking ▶

Cats can keep still for hours watching quietly for prey. When a cat spots a possible victim, it begins to stalk. Crouching low, with its head, body and tail held more or less level and its ears pricked, it glides silently forward.

Watching its prey intently, the cat starts to creep forward

◀ Freezing

When a cat gets close to its prey, it freezes low and prepares itself for the final dash and spring. Its bottom is raised up and begins to swing from side to side with the tip of its tail twitching with excitement.

Preparing for the final spring

Pouncing ▶

Finally, the cat plunges forward, pinning the prey down with its forepaws. Often the "prey" is just a leaf or some other small moving object, but if it is an animal, the cat kills it by biting it at the back of the neck.

The cat often plays with make-believe prey

The lips are drawn back like this in the Flehmen reaction

Showing friendship ▶

Cats use scent to show friendship and ownership. They mark people and objects with scent from glands on their head and tail, by rubbing up against them. People cannot smell this scent.

If a male cat is neutered when a few months old, it will be less likely to spray

◀ Flehmen reaction

Sense of smell is very important to cats. As well as smelling through the nose, they open their mouths and draw air into channels in the roof of the mouth which connect with a special scent organ. This is known as the Flehmen reaction.

◀ Marking territory

Male cats are very possessive about their home area or territory. They mark it out by backing up to objects and spraying them with drops of strong-smelling urine. The scent tells other cats "This is my territory."

Aggression and friendship

The cat may also growl and spit

◄ Aggression

A cat may take up this aggressive position if it feels threatened by another cat or a dog. The back is arched, the tail is held up stiffly and the fur stands on end. This makes the cat look much larger and helps to warn off enemies.

Ears are held back

Fear ►

A frightened cat will back off as far as possible if it is cornered by an enemy. Its eyes may dart about in search of an escape route and it may raise a warning paw, ready to strike out if the enemy moves forward.

◄ Friendship

Friendly cats greet each other by touching noses and whiskers, sniffing the forehead, lips and chin where there are scent glands.

Choosing a kitten

Think carefully before you get a kitten. Do not take one on impulse just because someone is trying to find a home for it, or because you see one looking sad in a pet shop. A cat is not a toy you can put aside if you get bored; most live to be at least ten years old. Food, cat litter and veterinary attention all cost money. You must also be prepared to arrange for someone to look after the cat when you go on vacation.

Once you have decided to have a cat of your own, you must think about what kind of cat you want. For example, longhaired cats need a lot of grooming; Siamese like company. The descriptions of breeds in this book will help you choose. If possible, get your kitten from the place where it was born rather than a pet store, so you can see that the mother cat is healthy and well cared for.

Healthy coat

Clean ears with no brown specks

Clean and dry under tail

Bright eyes

Clean nose

Full set of teeth

Sturdy limbs

Choose a healthy kitten

If you are out all day, consider having two kittens to keep each other company, especially if they are to be kept indoors.

Never choose a kitten that looks dirty or ill, or even an apparently healthy one from a litter where any others are sickly. The boldest kitten is not always the best choice, as it may become too confident and difficult to discipline. Choose a lively kitten that shows an interest in you, not one that is too shy.

Whether your choice is male or female doesn't really matter, because unless the cat is intended for breeding, it should have its sex organs removed by a vet when it is about five months old. This is called neutering (male cats) or spaying (female cats). If you don't do this with a female cat, you may find yourself with more kittens than you can find homes for. Un-neutered male cats, or toms, often get into fights, and will spray urine about their home to mark it as their territory.

Preparing for a new cat

Kittens can leave their mother when they are about eight weeks old. Before you bring your kitten home, make sure you get together the things it will need. The essentials are: a basket to carry it home in, a warm bed of its own, a plastic litter box and some cat litter, bowls for food and water, and some toys to play with. Have all cats and kittens examined by a vet before bringing them home, especially if you already have a cat.

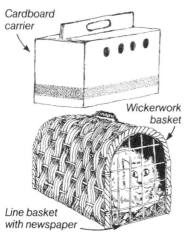

Cardboard carrier

Wickerwork basket

Line basket with newspaper

Carrying baskets

Carrying baskets are made in wickerwork, plastic-coated metal mesh, fiberglass and cardboard. The cardboard type are cheapest and fine or a kitten, but they do not last forever. A determined full-grown cat can force its way out.

Many cats like "windows" to look out of, but for a long journey or if the cat is sick, an enclosed basket is better as the cat will be more likely to sleep. Plastic-coated metal mesh and fiberglass baskets are easy to disinfect in case of sickness.

Whatever type of basket you choose, make sure it is strong and fastens securely, and has air holes.

A warm bed

You can make a comfortable bed for your kitten from a cardboard box. Cut a piece out on one side so the kitten can get in and out easily. Line the box with newspaper, with an old blanket on top. If it is very cold, a hot-water bottle wrapped in a blanket makes a good mother-substitute. Always wash the blanket and change the newspaper regularly.

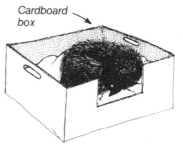

Cardboard box

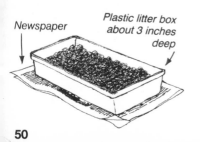

Newspaper

Plastic litter box about 3 inches deep

Litter box

The best litter boxes are made of plastic, which is easy to clean. Half-fill the box with dry cat litter, which you can buy from pet shops, and put it in a quiet corner. You should change the litter often; cats will not use a box that smells.

50

Cat collar

It is a good idea to get your kitten used to wearing a collar with an address tag if it is to be allowed outside when it is older. The collar must have an elastic section so that the cat will not get strangled if it gets caught on anything. If you take your cat on vacation with you, an address capsule is better than a tag, as you can put in a new slip of paper with your temporary address on.

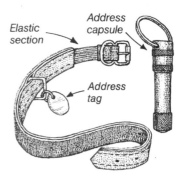

Elastic section • Address capsule • Address tag

Scratching post or pad

Unless trained not to, cats will sharpen their claws on furniture. You can prevent this by getting your kitten a scratching post or pad. Buy one at a pet shop, or make your own from a log with bark on or a stout post with burlap wrapped around. Your homemade post should be nailed to a piece of flat wood for a stand. Train the kitten to use the post by moving its paws up and down it a few times.

Cat flap

If you have a large yard, you can train your kitten to ask to go out instead of using a litter box as it gets older. Once it is trained, you could think about putting a cat flap in the back door. This is a good idea if you are out during the day, as it allows the cat to go in and out when it likes. In suburban areas and cities, however, you run the risk of exposing your cat to possible injury or disease.

Feeding your cat

Cats enjoy any kind of cooked meat and fish. Some starchy foods such as cereals help balance the diet, but not all cats will eat them. Fresh water should always be available. Most cats are quite happy to eat branded cat foods, which are made up from carefully balanced ingredients to provide a correct diet. These may come in a can, in dried form or in a moist form, sealed in a vacuum pack. Cats eating dried food *must* have plenty of water or they may have trouble urinating.

When you get a kitten, ask the owner what it has been fed, how often, and how much. Start off with what it is used to and introduce changes gradually. Kittens need plenty of calcium to make their bones grow strong. Special kitten formulas containing added calcium and protein are available in stores. Or you can supplement your kitten's diet with calcium supplied by your vet. Milk often causes diarrhea and can be difficult to digest.

Up to three months old: four small meals a day

Three to six months old: reduce to two meals a day

or

Over six months old: one big meal or two smaller ones a day

Never give kittens or cats ice-cold food straight from the refrigerator as it may cause stomach upsets. Remove small or brittle bones like those in fish and chicken, especially from cooked fish.

Kittens should be permitted to eat as much as they want. An adult cat normally needs 6-9 ounces of prepared cat food each day. This can be given as one big meal, or two smaller ones served morning and evening. Do not overfeed your cat. An average adult male cat weighs about 10 pounds and a female about 8 pounds. You can weigh your cat occasionally to make sure you are not overfeeding it, or try the rib test shown here.

Cats like grass; they cannot digest it but it gives them roughage (like bran for people). It also helps them bring up fur swallowed when grooming. So if you do not have a garden, grow some grass in a pot.

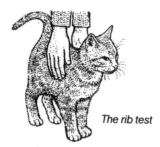

The rib test

Place your fingers over your cat's ribs like this. If the cat is the right weight for its size, you should be able to feel all its ribs by pressing lightly.

Training your cat

It is important to establish firm rules for your cat right from the start, when you bring it home as a young kitten. Cats become confused if they are allowed to do something one day and forbidden to do it the next.

Let your cat know right away where it is allowed to go. Do not let it jump up onto kitchen worktops or onto a stove, where it might get burned. Decide whether you want to ban your cat from any rooms, such as bedrooms, and keep to your rule.

A kitten's mother usually teaches it to use a litter box. If your kitten has not been trained, be ready to pick it up and put it on its litter box at the first sign that it wants to relieve itself. Praise your kitten when it uses the box. If it forgets, and you see it go elsewhere, scold it and put it on the box, but there is no point scolding it for puddles discovered later.

Whenever your kitten makes a mess on the floor, you should clean the spot at once with disinfectant.

Otherwise, the smell will remain and encourage the kitten to go there again.

There is little point in punishing an adult cat that relieves itself in the wrong place. If the cat is normally well-trained, this is probably a sign that something is wrong. The cat may be ill, for example, or you may have forgotten to change the litter in its litter box (cats are very clean animals and will not use a wet or dirty box). Cats occasionally urinate in the wrong place as a protest about a change in routine that is upsetting them.

Train your cat by praising it and scolding it. Your tone of voice should normally be enough to let it know what you mean. A tap on a cat's nose with your finger is the nearest you should ever get to hitting it. Physical punishment never works well with cats; but you can try behavior modification. For instance, to keep your cat off a counter you could (gently) spray it in the face with a plant mister, *but don't let it see you doing that*. Then it will associate walking on the counter with something unpleasant.

A cat usually runs to greet its owner with its tail held up like this

Calling your cat

Give your cat a short name it can easily recognize. Call it to you by name, or by whistling or clicking your tongue. When it comes, make a fuss of it to show how pleased you are. Many cats soon recognize their owners' footsteps (or the sound of their car engines) and run to meet them when they come home.

Grooming your cat

All cats need regular grooming. It helps keep their coat in good condition and stops them from swallowing too much fur when they wash. Shorthaired cats should be groomed at least once a week, and longhaired cats every day. It is best to use a bristle brush and a metal comb. Get your kitten used to them right away so it is not frightened and will enjoy being groomed. Even stroking, which all cats enjoy, helps to remove loose fur and gives a shine to the cat's coat.

If a longhaired cat's coat gets matted despite regular grooming cut the lumps of fur out carefully with scissors.

Cats do not normally need bathing because they wash their fur frequently with their very rough tongues. An elderly or sick cat may wash itself less often, however, and you should therefore give its coat extra attention.

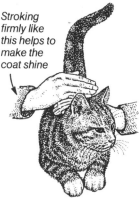

Stroking firmly like this helps to make the coat shine

Shaking its head and brown specks in its ears may mean ear mites

Scratching may mean fleas

When you groom your cat, check that its ears are clean and free from ear mites and that there are no signs of fleas. Cat fleas are found most often around a cat's neck and head. Look for dark, dirt-like specks in the fur which are flea droppings. Your vet or a pet shop will have a powder or spray for treating fleas, and the vet will give you drops for ear mites. Always follow the instructions on the container very carefully.

Games and toys

Kittens develop their hunting and fighting skills by playing together. When you take your new kitten home, away from its mother, you must take the place of its former playmates.

A cat can spend hours playing on its own or with another cat, but particularly enjoys a game in which its owner takes part, even if he or she is only holding and twitching the other end of a piece of string. Cats can have a lot of fun with simple toys, such as empty thread spools, paper bags and balls of crumpled paper or aluminium foil. They also love chasing and pouncing games.

Cats usually chase only moving objects, and are unlikely to play with electric wires. However, do not let your cat play with wires or plugs. If it were to bite through one, it would kill itself. Also, avoid toys made of, or covered with, plastic or sponge rubber that a cat might chew and swallow.

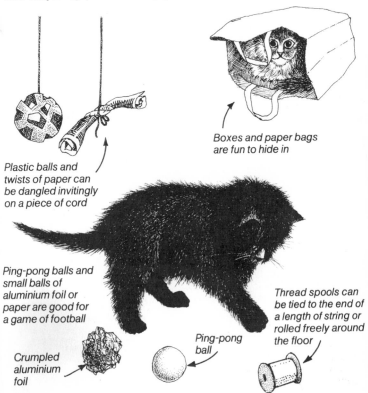

Boxes and paper bags are fun to hide in

Plastic balls and twists of paper can be dangled invitingly on a piece of cord

Ping-pong balls and small balls of aluminium foil or paper are good for a game of football

Crumpled aluminium foil

Ping-pong ball

Thread spools can be tied to the end of a length of string or rolled freely around the floor

Your cat's health

A cat that is ill looks listless and may refuse to eat, or be sick after eating. Its coat may look harsh and messy, and it may have diarrhea. Another sign of possible ill-health is when you can see the cat's nictitating membrane or "third eyelid" at the corner of its eye.

Vomiting is not necessarily a serious sign. Cats are sometimes sick if they have eaten their food too quickly, or if they need to get rid of a fur ball (see page 43). Bad food can cause diarrhea; going without food for a day may cure the cat.

Take your cat to the vet if it has trouble relieving itself and seems constipated, or if its sickness or diarrhea continue for more than a day. If you are in any doubt about your cat's health, take it to the vet anyway. Young kittens must be taken to a vet to be vaccinated against feline distemper and respiratory infection, which can kill cats. They need a booster shot each year.

Parasites

Roundworms and tapeworms are internal parasites that many cats pick up. They should be treated by a veterinarian. You may see roundworms moving about in your cat's vomit if it is sick. Tapeworms are made up of segments shaped like grains of rice; you may see one under your cat's tail. Kittens with worms often look pot-bellied.

Collect a sample of your cat's vomit or solid waste, put it in a container and take it with you when you take your cat to the vet. This will help the vet find out if your cat has worms.

Fleas and mites are external parasites. They are easy to get rid of if noticed early (see page 53).

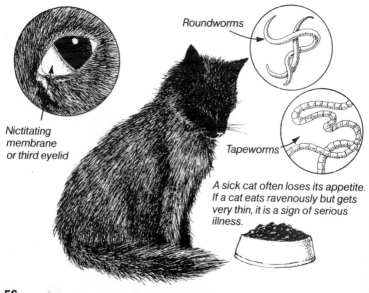

Roundworms

Nictitating membrane or third eyelid

Tapeworms

A sick cat often loses its appetite. If a cat eats ravenously but gets very thin, it is a sign of serious illness.

Caring for a sick cat

If your cat is ill, give it a comfortable bed in a quiet, warm place, away from bright lights, drafts and noise. Reassure it, but don't fuss over it too much.

Follow the vet's instructions on care, feeding and medicine very carefully. Help your cat to keep clean, and change its bedding if it becomes soiled. Leave fresh water and a litter box within easy reach of its bed.

Cats usually recover very quickly from cuts and minor injuries. But because they heal so rapidly, dirt and foreign bodies are sometimes sealed inside the wound, where they may cause an infection. It is best to have wounds treated by a vet, who can clean the wound thoroughly, and stitch it up if necessary.

You should learn how to give your cat pills and medicines. Liquid

Gently pull out the skin at the side of the cat's mouth and rest the eye-dropper between its front and back teeth to squirt in liquid medicine.

medicine can be given using an eye-dropper or plastic syringe. Mix powders up with your cat's food. If you need to be sure that the cat has had the whole dose, mix up the powder in some liquid and give it like medicine; or mix it in a spoonful of cream, which most cats will think a treat. Pills should be given in the way shown below.

Giving a pill

1

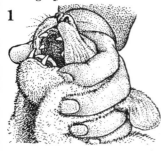

Get someone to hold the cat still. Hold the top of its head with one hand, tilting it back as you do so, and gently squeeze the sides of its mouth with your thumb and first finger. This makes the mouth open. Pop in the pill, as far back as you can.

2

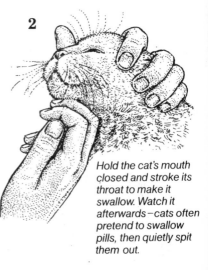

Hold the cat's mouth closed and stroke its throat to make it swallow. Watch it afterwards – cats often pretend to swallow pills, then quietly spit them out.

Pedigree cats and shows

There are many organizations around the world that are concerned with breeding and showing pedigree cats. In the United States and Canada there are several such bodies operating independently. These are the associations for most breeds of cats – Siamese, Longhairs, and so forth. In addition there are larger organizations that sponsor shows, maintain stud book registries, and publish bulletins, newsletters, and books (see page 60).

You can look in local newspapers and cat magazines for details of cat shows organized by the official body or by cat clubs. You may see lots of interesting cats even at local pet shows.

If you would like to exhibit your own cat in a show, apply to the organizers for an entry form and a list of rules. Many shows include classes for non-pedigree cats in which ordinary pet cats may be entered.

Since your cat may have to travel some distance to the show, and then spend all day in its show cage, make sure it is used to its carrying basket, and that it will not become upset if kept cooped up for a long time.

Pedigree kittens are registered by the breeder, that is, the owner of the mother cat. If you arrange to buy a pedigree kitten that has not yet been registered, you may be able to choose a name for it. You will have to give several alternatives, because many owners choose the same names for their cats.

If you intend to breed from your kitten, or to show it yourself, apply to the official body for the ownership of the kitten to be changed to your own name. The seller should give you a signed transfer form.

If you do not want to breed from your cat, you should have it spayed or neutered (see page 49).

Glossary

Bi-color – cat with a coat that is white and one other color. Not more than two-thirds of the coat should be colored and not more than one-half white in show standard cats.

Cobby – sturdy body set on short, sturdy legs, as in Longhair cats.

Persian – another name for a Longhair cat.

Queen – an un-neutered female cat.

Self – cat of a single overall color.

Tom – an un-neutered male cat.

Type – the main characteristics that distinguish each breed and identify it as a Shorthair, Longhair or Foreign cat.

Vibrissae – whiskers and eyebrows: the pressure-sensitive hairs on a cat's face.

Whisker pads – muscular pads from which the whiskers grow.

Illness and injury

Constipation – blocked bowels, due to lack of exercise, swallowing a lot of fur, or drinking too little. The cat finds it difficult or impossible to excrete solid waste.

Diarrhea – a condition of the intestine that makes cats excrete frequently. Their solid waste is runny. See also page 56.

Ear mites – tiny, white parasites found in cats' ears that cause a black discharge. They make cats scratch around their ears and shake their head. See also page 54.

Feline distemper – a dangerous virus that can kill cats and must be treated by a veterinarian at once. A cat with this disease suddenly becomes miserable, then starts to vomit. It loses weight rapidly and will die if not treated. All cats should be vaccinated against this disease.

Fleas – common parasites that live on cats' bodies and suck their blood. Cat fleas do not live on people. See also page 54.

Fur balls – fur swallowed during washing that collects in a mass in a cat's stomach. Fur balls are common in the spring, when cats are molting, and longhaired cats are especially likely to suffer from them. Frequent brushing helps.

Rabies – a painful and usually fatal disease carried by many animals. A cat with rabies hides away for a few days, then becomes paralyzed and dies. It may become aggressive for a while before it dies. A person bitten by an animal with rabies usually dies.

Road accidents – if a cat gets run over, it should be gently lifted onto a coat or into a box, covered with a blanket and taken to a vet.

Roundworms – parasites that live inside a cat's body and suck its blood. Roundworms cause loss of condition and sometimes diarrhea. They are common in kittens.

Tapeworms – long, whitish parasites made up of segments. They bury their heads in cats' bowels. Tapeworms cause indigestion and loss of condition. Fleas carry tapeworms. See also page 56.

Upper respiratory infection – an infectious virus that causes sneezing, watery or streaming eyes and a blocked nose; should be vaccinated against.

Useful addresses

American Cat Fanciers Association, P.O. Box 203, Point Lookout, MO 65726; (417) 334-5430. Founded in 1955; 163 local groups. Breeders and exhibitors of purebred cats; maintains stud book registry; publishes monthly bulletin.

American Feline Society, 204 W. 20th St. New York, NY 10011. Founded in 1938 to alleviate cat suffering and abuse; rescue stray cats; and provide information on cat history, care, and feeding to the general public.

Cat Fanciers Association, 1805 Atlantic Ave. P.O. Box 1005 Manasquan, NJ 08736-0805; (908) 528-9797. Founded in 1908. A federation of all-breed and specialty cat clubs; promotes welfare of cats, registers pedigrees, and licenses shows held under association rules.

Cat Fanciers' Federation, 9509 Montgomery Rd. Cincinatti, OH 45242 (513) 984-1841. Founded in 1919. A federation of local clubs of people who own, breed, and exhibit cats, and who are interested in the general welfare of cats. The federation maintains records on the ancestry of cats, encourages shows, trains judges, and so forth. Local clubs hold annual shows, under Federation rules, usually for the benefit of humane organizations.

Canadian Cat Association, Suite 5, 14 Nelson Street, West, Brampton, Ontario.

Books to read

Understanding Cats. Bridget Gibbs (Hayes Books). A paperback packed with information about the behavior, care, and training of cats. Lots of color illustrations.

The Silent Miaow. Paul Gallico and Suzanne Szasz (Crown). A manual for kittens, strays, and homeless cats – from going to the vet to speech, travelling, and motherhood – all told from the cat's point of view. A wonderful book; illustrated with over 200 candid photos.

The New Basic Book of the Cat. William Carr (Scribners). An all-purpose book that discusses breed standards, how to prepare for shows, and first aid.

Understanding Your Cat. Dr. Michael Fox (Bantam). A handy paperback guide to living happily with your cat; mostly discusses cat behavior.

Pat Widmer's Cat Book. Patricia Widmer (Scribners). Subtitled "straight talk for city and suburban cat owners," includes information on housebreaking, declawing, care and feeding, and behavior. Photos.

Pictorial Encyclopedia of Cats. Grace Pond (Rand McNally). The history and behavior of cats, choosing a cat, and cat shows. A large book with a lot of photos, many in color.

Cat Fancy, 11760 Sorrento Valley Road, San Diego, CA 92121; bimonthly magazine.

Cats Magazine, P.O. Box 4106, Pittsburgh, PA 15202; monthly.

Scorecard

The cats in this scorecard are arranged in alphabetical order. When you spot a particular breed, fill in the date next to its name. You can add up your score after a day out spotting.

	Score	Date seen		Score	Date seen
Abyssinian, Blue	20		Bombay	30	
Abyssinian, Lilac	25		British Blue	10	
Abyssinian, Normal or Ruddy	10		British Tipped Shorthair	25	
Abyssinian, Red or Sorrel	15		Brown Tabby and White (longhaired)	5	
American Wirehair	30		Brown Tabby and White (shorthaired)	5	
Balinese (any colour)	25		Burmese, Blue	10	
Bi-color Longhair, Black and White	5		Burmese, Blue-Cream	20	
Bi-color Longhair, Blue and White	15		Burmese, Brown	10	
Bi-color Longhair, Cream and White	15		Burmese, Chocolate	15	
Bi-color Longhair, Red and White	5		Burmese, Chocolate Tortie	20	
Bi-color Shorthair, Black and White	5		Burmese, Cream	20	
Bi-color Shorthair, Blue and White	15		Burmese, Lilac	20	
Bi-color Shorthair, Cream and White	15		Burmese, Red	15	
Bi-color Shorthair, Red and White	5		Cameo, Shaded	25	
Birman, Blue-point	25		Cameo, Shell	25	
Birman, Seal-point	25		Cameo, Smoke or Red Smoke	25	
Black Longhair	5		Chinchilla	15	
Black Shorthair	5		Cream Longhair	10	
Blue Longhair	10		Cream Shorthair	10	
Blue-Cream Longhair	15		Cymric	30	
Blue-Cream Shorthair	15		Exotic Shorthair	30	

	Score	Date seen		Score	Date seen
Foreign Black	15		Siamese, Blue-point	10	
Foreign Lilac	15		Siamese, Chocolate-point	10	
Foreign White	10		Siamese, Cream-point	20	
Havana	15		Siamese, Lilac-point	15	
Himalayan, Blue-point	15		Siamese, Red-point	15	
Himalayan, Chocolate-point	10		Siamese, Seal-point	5	
Himalayan, Cream-point	20		Siamese, Tabby-point	20	
Himalayan, Flame-point	10		Siamese, Tortie-point	15	
Himalayan, Lilac-point	15		Silver Tabby and White (longhaired)	5	
Himalayan, Seal-point	15		Silver Tabby and White (shorthaired)	5	
Himalayan, Tortie-point	15		Smoke Longhair, Black	20	
Japanese Bobtail	30		Smoke Longhair, Blue	15	
Korat	20		Smoke Shorthair	25	
Maine Coon	15		Somali	30	
Manx, Rumpy	15		Sphynx	30	
Manx, Stumpy	15		Spotted Shorthair, Brown	15	
Oriental Spotted Tabby (any color)	25		Spotted Shorthair, Cream	25	
Red Self Longhair	10		Spotted Shorthair, Red	20	
Red Tabby and White (longhaired)	5		Spotted Shorthair, Silver	15	
Red Tabby and White (shorthaired)	5		Tabby Longhair, Brown	15	
Rex, Cornish	15		Tabby Longhair, Red	10	
Rex, Devon	15		Tabby Longhair, Silver	15	
Russian Blue	10		Tabby Shorthair, Brown Classic	10	
Scottish Fold	30		Tabby Shorthair, Brown Mackerel	10	
Si-Rex (any color)	20		Tabby Shorthair, Red Classic	10	

	Score	Date seen		Score	Date seen
abby Shorthair, Red Mackerel	10		Hunting, pouncing	5	
abby Shorthair, Silver Classic	10		Jumping down	5	
abby Shorthair, Silver Mackerel	10		Jumping up	5	
ortoiseshell Longhair	10		Marking territory	20	
ortoiseshell Shorthair	5		Sharpening claws	5	
ortoiseshell and White Longhair	10		Sleeping	5	
ortoiseshell and White Shorthair	5		Stretching, arching back	10	
Turkish Cat	25		Stretching, back legs	5	
White Longhair, Blue-eyed	10		Stretching, front legs	5	
White Longhair, Odd-eyed	15		Touch (sense of)	10	
White Longhair, Orange-eyed	10		Washing, face and ears	5	
White Shorthair, Blue-eyed	10		Washing, hindquarters	5	
White Shorthair, Odd-eyed	15		Washing, side of body	5	
White Shorthair, Orange-eyed	10				
					•

Cat behavior

	Score	Date seen
Aggression	20	
Climbing	5	
Eating grass	10	
Fear	20	
Flehmen reaction	15	
Friendship (to other cats)	15	
Friendship (to people)	15	
Hunting, stalking	5	
Hunting, freezing	5	

Index